# Space
# Shuttle

Experts on child reading levels
have consulted on the level of text and
concepts in this book.

At the end of the book is a "Look Back and Find" section
which provides additional information and encourages
the child to refer back to previous pages
for the answers to the questions posed.

Angela Grunsell trained as a teacher in 1969.
She has a Diploma in Reading and Related Skills
and for the last five years has advised London
teachers on materials and resources.
She works for the ILEA as an advisory teacher in
primary schools in Hackney, London.

*Published in the United States in 1984 by*
Franklin Watts, 387 Park Avenue South, New York, NY 10016

© Aladdin Books Ltd/Franklin Watts

*Designed and produced by*
Aladdin Books Ltd, 70 Old Compton Street, London W1

ISBN 0-531-04812-8

*Printed in Belgium*

FRANKLIN · WATTS · FIRST · LIBRARY

# Space Shuttle

by
Kate Petty

Consultant
Angela Grunsell

Illustrated by
Tessa Barwick

Franklin Watts
London · New York · Toronto · Sydney

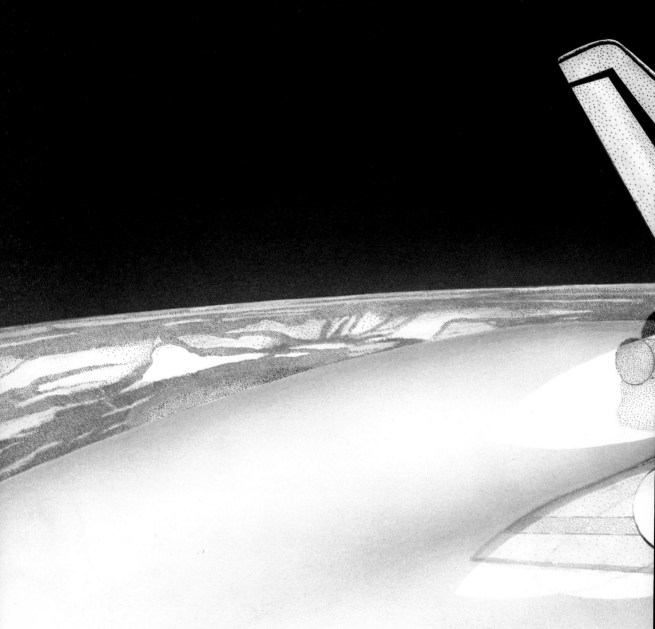

Would you like to take a trip into space one day?
This could really happen in your lifetime.

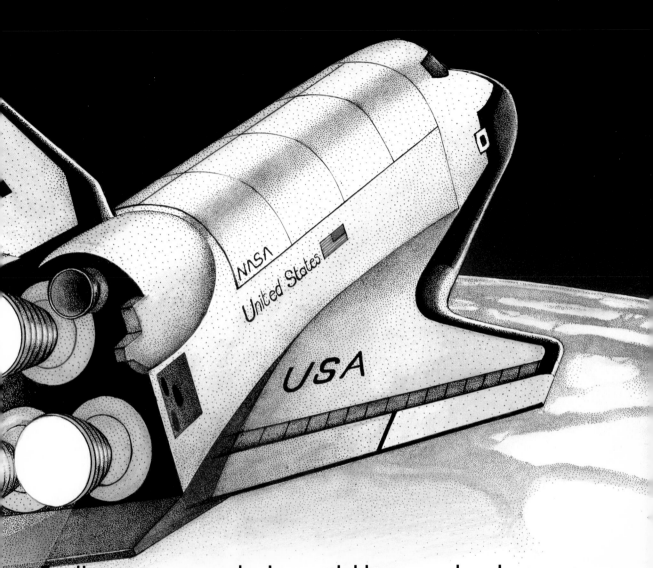

Earlier space rockets could be used only once. A space shuttle can "shuttle" to and from space many times. How does it work?

The space shuttle travels on the back of a jumbo jet.
At the launch site it is joined to the rockets
which will lift it into space.

The astronauts feel excited as they set off for the shuttle, at last, after their months of training.

"3-2-1. Ignition. Lift-off!" The three engines
and two rocket boosters lift the space shuttle
into the sky. The enormous tank carries fuel.

10

In only two minutes the shuttle is 28 miles (45 km) from the Earth. The burned-out rocket boosters fall away from the shuttle.

Six minutes later the fuel tank is empty too.
It is ejected and breaks into bits
as it falls to Earth.

What has happened to the rocket boosters?

They are parachuting toward the sea.

They are towed back to base by ship.

Just eleven minutes after lift-off the shuttle is in space. Two small engines are fired to set it going in orbit around the Earth.

The doors of the cargo bay stay open
in space to keep the shuttle cool.
One orbit around the Earth takes
one and a half hours.

On the flight deck there are over 2,000 knobs and dials. The astronauts read the information they need from TV screens.

If anything goes wrong, an alarm sounds
in their headsets. A button lights up
to show where the problem is.

The crew is spending seven days in the shuttle.
Because they are weightless in space
they must strap themselves in to sleep.

The astronauts fit their feet into footholds
on the floor so they don't float about.
They make meals from prepacked food.

The astronaut must put on a space suit to go outside.
Under his helmet is a cap containing headphones
which is nicknamed a "snoopy cap."

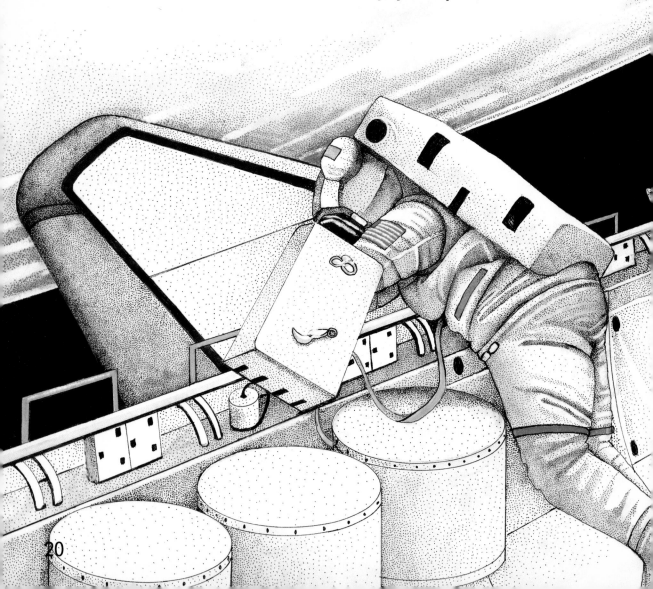

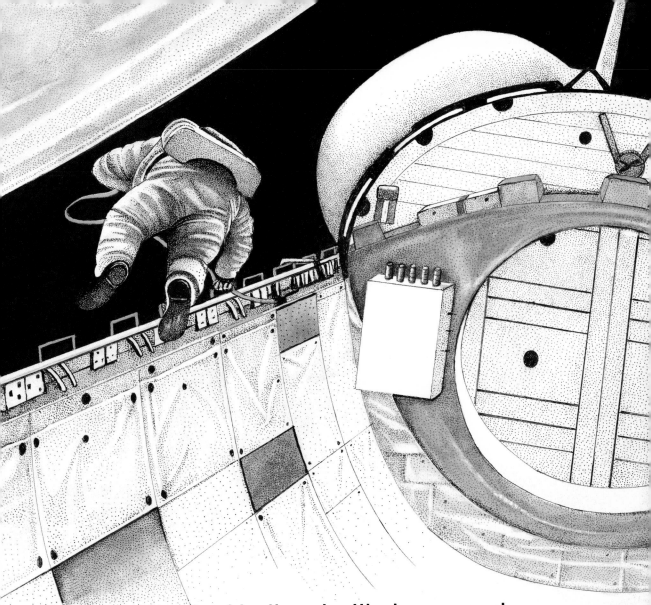

He is connected to the shuttle by a cord
to stop him drifting away. On future trips
astronauts may wear jet thrusters instead.

This shuttle is carrying parts for a satellite.
The astronaut is working a robot arm
to unload the parts from the cargo bay.

She watches the movements of the robot arm on a screen on the flight deck. Soon the shuttle will be ready to return to Earth.

The shuttle is slowed down to bring it out of orbit. The heatproof tiles on the bottom glow red-hot when it reenters the Earth's atmosphere.

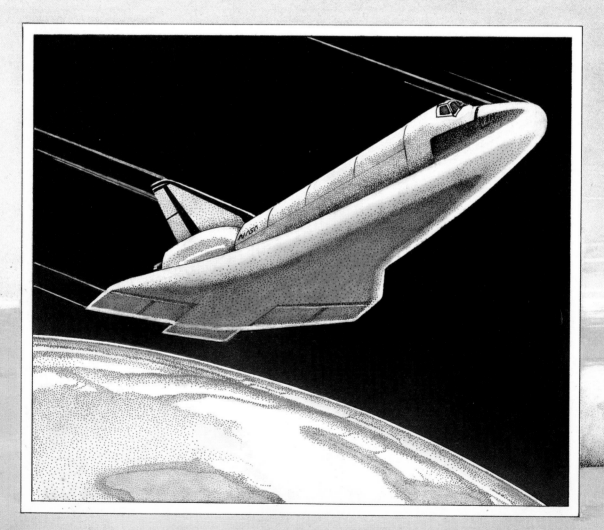

This homeward journey is made with no power at all. The shuttle glides a fifth of the way around the Earth before landing.

Within a week the shuttle can be ready
to take off again.

In a few years the shuttle may be used
to build a space station. You might be able
to travel there in the shuttle or even further
to a space city beyond.

# Look back and find

What is the big difference between the space shuttle and earlier rockets?

Why does this make space travel more possible for you?
*Because it is much cheaper.*

The fastest car can travel 5.58 miles (9 km) in two minutes. How far from Earth is the shuttle two minutes after lift-off?

What happens to the fuel tank?
*It falls into the ocean.*

What happens to the boosters?

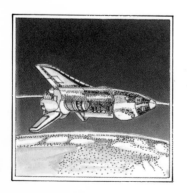

How far away is space?
*The Earth's atmosphere ends 124 miles (200 km) above the Earth.*

What is the main difference between the Earth's atmosphere and space?
*There is no air in space and no gravity.*

Why do people seem to have no weight in space?
*Because they are too far away to feel
the pull of Earth's gravity.*

How do they stop themselves from
floating about?

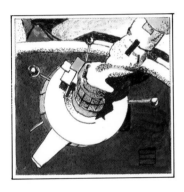

What was the cargo on this trip?

How can the shuttle help scientists do
experiments in space?
*A laboratory called "spacelab"
can be fitted into the cargo bay
and taken up into space.*

Why do the heatproof tiles glow red-hot?
*The shuttle strikes the air of Earth's
atmosphere at tremendous speed.
The friction between them makes
the shuttle hot.*

How does the shuttle come down?

# Index

PRINTED IN BELGIUM BY

INTERNATIONAL BOOK PRODUCTION